DETROIT TODAY
A Portrait in Color

Photographed by D. E. Cox

A&M
Altwerger and Mandel Publishing Company, West Bloomfield, Michigan

Above, Wayne State University's Minoru Yamasaki–designed College of Education Building.

Cover, Cobo Conference/Exhibition Center's striking geometric facade.

Page 1, Mary Chase Stratton's Pewabic Pottery tile work, *Progress,* graces the entrance to downtown's art deco-style Guardian Building.

Pages 2–3, boaters on the Detroit River at dusk anticipate the annual International Freedom Festival fireworks spectacular.

Copyright © 1991 by D. E. Cox. All rights are reserved. No part of this book can be reproduced in any form or by any means without permission by writing the author or publisher.

First Edition, 1991.

ISBN 1-878005-29-4

Designed by Mary Primeau

Enlargements and limited editions of the photographs as well as autographed copies of the book can be obtained by writing to the publisher or by telephoning 313-561-1842.

A&M Publishing Company
6346 Orchard Lake Road, Suite 201
West Bloomfield, Michigan 48033
Printed in Singapore through Palace Press

FOREWORD

Mention Detroit to most out-of-towners and certain epithets immediately surface: Motown, the Motor City, and the Murder City. Probe further and Detroit is too frequently designated a symbol of American cities in crisis. Whatever happened to those more favorable appelations of the City of Churches, the Arsenal of Democracy, the City of Progress, and the Renaissance City?

The images evoked by photographer Dennis Cox in **Detroit Today** reveal another Detroit—a city very much alive and kicking. True, the city suffers from many of the ills of modern life, but these problems in no way should exclusively define life in greater metropolitan Detroit today. The color images in this book present a more vital and energetic side of the city.

We invite both Detroit's critics and boosters to an incredible feast of color photographs capturing **Detroit Today**—a Detroit that Detroiters fondly call "our hometown."

—*The Publishers*

Framed by a lobby skylight, the Westin Hotel's soaring 72-story tower (above) is the centerpiece of the Renaissance Center.

From Philip A. Hart Civic Center Plaza, Isamu Noguchi's Horace A. Dodge and Son Memorial Fountain and John Portman's Renaissance Center (right) appear to be one work of sculpture around which little girls and rainbows frolic.

Strung like pearls across the Detroit River, the lights of the 1.8 mile-long Ambassador Bridge link Detroit with her "southern" Canadian neighbor, the city of Windsor, Ontario. Opened in 1929, the Ambassador Bridge is the world's longest international suspension bridge.

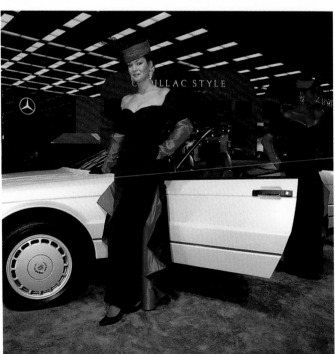

The refurbished 19th century Wayne County Building (left) stands in contrast to its modern neighbors, the Millender Center and Renaissance Center.

Since Henry Ford built his first model in 1896, Fords, like the one above at Greenfield Village's Old Car Festival, have been rolling out of Detroit.

The modern auto industry's glitz and glamour (right) is displayed annually at the North American International Auto Show at Cobo Center.

Amid a flurry of sparks on the robotic welding line of Chrysler's Sterling Heights Assembly Plant (left), a new Plymouth takes shape.

The international character of today's automotive industry is symbolized in the graphic silhouette of a fully loaded car carrier crossing the Ambassador Bridge (above).

Kids and other superheroes hang out at the Detroit Science Center (above) and descend the colorful escalator (left) to experience the thrilling presentations in the center's Omnimax Space Theatre.

A young student of the Detroit—Windsor Dance Academy (above) relaxes at the Paradigm Center for the Arts in downtown Harmonie Park.

The gardens of Cranbrook's 1908 English Manor House (right) display over 5,000 annuals as the centerpiece of the 325-acre educational community in Bloomfield Hills.

Following pages, highlight of the annual International Freedom Festival celebration, the fireworks extravaganza draws enormous crowds to both banks of the Detroit River.

Detroit is one of only four cities in the world with an operating double-deck trolley (above). The others are Blackpool, England; Cairo, Egypt; and Hong Kong.

Suburban Northville's Main Street (right) harks back to a simpler time.

Since 1892, historic, open-air Eastern Market has been the colorful scene for buying and selling fresh produce (left). In May, the market attracts flower growers from around Michigan and other states for the annual Flower Show (above).

Among six murals executed for the Detroit People Mover system by Pewabic Pottery is Tom Phardel's *In Honor of W. Hawkins Ferry* (left) at the Times Square station. J. Seward Johnson's bronze figure, *Catching Up* (above), reads a combined Detroit News and Detroit Free Press waiting for the People Mover at the Grand Circus Park station.

The "thunderboats"—unlimited hydroplanes (above)—make their appearance on the Detroit River each June for the Detroit Gold Cup race.

On a more tranquil note, a canoe (right) glides through the lagoon of nearby Belle Isle, America's largest urban island park.

Henry Ford Museum's *The Automobile in American Life* display (opposite) chronicles the country's car culture.

The annual Michigan State Fair, in September, provides a fantasyland on the midway for children (above) and such family entertainment as Kowalski's famous racing, or sometimes just waddling, pigs (left).

Detroit's city playgrounds (above) are where dreams are born of someday appearing on "Palacevision" (right) before a crowd of cheering Pistons fans at the Palace of Auburn Hills.

Hot jazz on a hot summer night results in a cool jam session (above) during the annual Montreux—Detroit International Jazz Festival. Featured are international jazz greats and local stars, such as the New McKinney Cotton Pickers (right), shown leading a parade through Hart Plaza to kick off the Labor Day weekend event.

All eyes, and many cameras (above), focus on the world's top racing drivers as they speed through the city during the internationally acclaimed Detroit Grand Prix in June.

Also commanding the attention of visitors to the city, the Renaissance Center (right) dominates Detroit's skyline with six office towers and one of the world's tallest hotels.

The open spaces of northern Oakland County, such as Independence Oaks County Park (above), provide solace from the city on a pleasant autumn afternoon.

Contemplation of form and space is also inspired by the sculpture garden (right) on the campus of Oakland University in Rochester.

Free after-work concerts in the minipark across from General Motors World Headquarters (above) are popular with New Center office workers.

Most Detroiters, it seems, love their Coney Islands—hot dogs smothered with chili, mustard, and onions—at any hour of the day or night at the American or Lafayette downtown.

Lazy summer days in Detroit are perfect for a trip to the Detroit Zoo (above) in Royal Oak, a "summer polish" on the van at Belle Isle Park (right), or a day of boating on Lake St. Clair out of Jefferson Beach Marina (opposite).

Wintertime events and activities in metropolitan Detroit include the Plymouth Ice Sculpture Spectacular (above), where more than 200 frozen figures of all shapes and sizes are featured, and ice skating (right) on amphitheater rink of downtown's Philip A. Hart Civic Center Plaza.

WASHINGTON

Flanked by a statue of George Washington in downtown Detroit, the Gothic stone Old Mariners' Church (left) has ministered to Great Lakes sailors since 1849.

Dearborn's Henry Ford Museum and Greenfield Village provides an extensive calendar of special events throughout the year including the annual Old Car Festival (above) featuring hundreds of antique automobiles from the turn of the century through 1929.

A Golden Family is raised aloft in the palm of Marshall Frederick's city symbol, *The Spirit of Detroit* (above), at the City-County Building. Nearby, the classically elegant lines of Giacomo Manzu's bronze *Passo DiDanza (Step of the Dance)* (right) are highlighted by the morning sun.

Colorful sails line the shore of Lake St. Clair at Metropolitan Beach Metropark (above), 770 acres near Mt. Clemens providing many recreational activities.

Entertainment in the heart of Detroit focuses on Philip A. Hart Civic Center Plaza, a 10-acre "people place" featuring an extensive series of Riverfront Festivals as well as a mime or two (right).

Named for the city's most famous sports hero, the beloved "Brown Bomber," Joe Louis Arena (right) is the downtown home of Red Wings hockey, Turbos lacrosse, Drive football, boxing, and other sports.

The Prudential Town Center complex (above), noted for the golden facades of its key buildings, marks suburban Southfield's downtown.

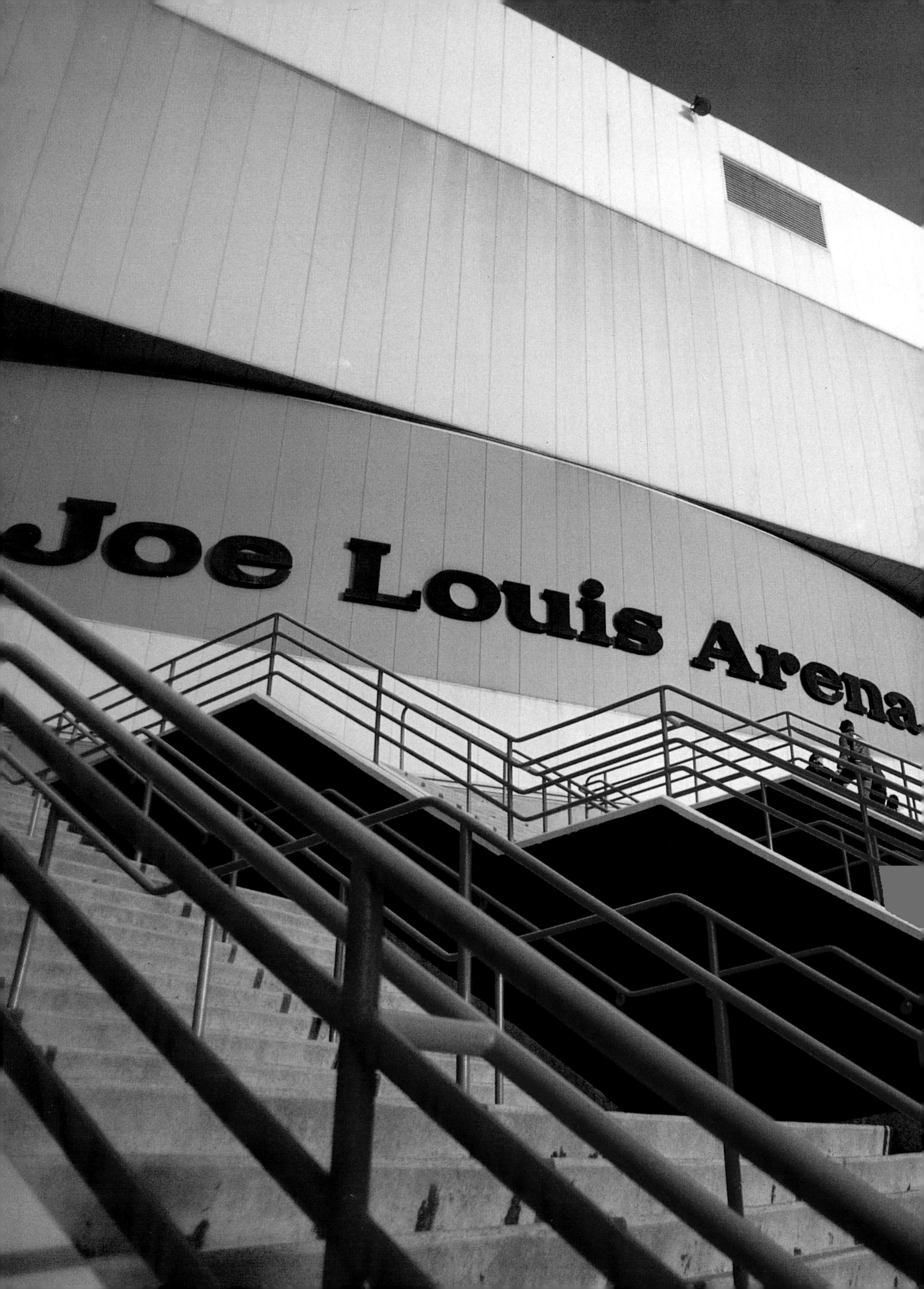
Joe Louis Arena

One of the historic homes of the auto barons, the Cotswold Estate of Edsel and Eleanor Ford in Grosse Pointe Shores (above) is preserved as a museum that hosts occasional special events and exhibits.

The golden roof of the Albert Kahn-designed Fisher Building (seen at right through the archway entrance to the General Motors Building) has dominated the New Center area since its completion in 1928.

Birmingham's quaint Pierce Street (above) is typical of shopping areas in Detroit's older suburbs, which feature specialty shops, galleries, and friendly little bistros tucked away from the bustle of the malls.

Masterfully designed to blend into its surroundings, the 150 West Jefferson (Madden) Building (right) constructively contributes to the evolving skyline of downtown Detroit.

In an impromptu jam session along the Detroit River at Chene Park, three jazz musicians (above) echo the spirit of the city with their drums.

Detroit's rich ethnic diversity is reflected by the Polish-Americans from throughout the metropolitan area (right), who annually march in the Hamtramck Festival Parade.

Known internationally for its superior acoustics, historic Orchestra Hall (above) was built in 1914 as the home of the Detroit Symphony.

Since 1925 the Vermont white marble of the restored James Scott Fountain (right) has been a Belle Isle landmark attracting visitors with its 109 water spouts and ever changing multicolored lights.

Spring plowing from an earlier era (left) takes place on the Firestone Farm—original Ohio home of the tire magnate—at Henry Ford Museum and Greenfield Village in Dearborn. America's largest indoor/outdoor museum, its extensive collection of Americana (above) fills 260 acres and includes the historic homes and workshops of several famous Americans.

Following pages, the downtown skywalk connecting Millender Center and the City−County Building provide protection for pedestrians from inclement weather.

Detroiters are drawn to their riverfront to watch the passing freighters (top) or to board the classic old steamers SS *St. Clair* and SS *Columbia* (above) for a trip downstream to Boblo Island park. Ships from around the Great Lakes and around the world dock at the Port of Detroit (right).

CYCLAMEN
INDICUM

The flowers bloom year-round at the Anna Scripps Whitcomb Conservatory on Belle Isle (left) and are most popular around the holiday season.

A wintry evening in Pontiac often finds a stream of traffic heading to the Silverdome (above), the nation's largest air-suspended domed stadium, for Lions football, concerts, conventions, and other special events.

Following page, The Greektown Art Fair is cast aglow on a spring evening by the multicolored neon sculpture of Stephen Antonakos affixed to the Greektown People Mover station.